I|N|D|I|F|F|E|R|E|N|T C|I|T|I|E|S

THE HELENA WHITEHILL AWARD

Sally Whitehill, an extraordinarily generous member of the Tupelo Press Board of Directors, has underwritten an annual book prize in honor of her mother, Helena Whitehill, for manuscripts of poetry as well as works of creative nonfiction, including memoir, essays, and hybrid texts.

Sally Whitehill writes: My mother, Helena Whitehill, loved words, and in particular, poetry. She believed creative expression should and could be for everybody, and passed this belief on to me and to my sisters. In Tupelo Press and Jeffrey Levine, I am excited to find partners who share this doctrine. The anonymous nature of the submission process for the Helena Whitehill Book Award is one way we have put this belief into action. I can think of no better way to honor my mother than to support this prize and other writers.

The Helena Whitehill Book Award includes a cash award of $1,000 in addition to publication by Tupelo Press, a book launch, national and international distribution by the University of Chicago Press, and a one-week residency at Gentle House on the Olympic Peninsula.

"Ángel García's *Indifferent Cities* has the feel of an epic journey: a quest for a return, to find a family, to find a name, a history, an identity. Along the way, the poet's multilingual documentations of the diasporic Americas suggest that movement is both a politics and a poetics: where not knowing is an epistemological position that is central to the experience of trying to understand how the forces of history have shaped who you are and what your body and words might become."

—Daniel Borzutzky, winner of the National Book Award for Poetry

"*Indifferent Cities* traces a relentless search—for names, for language itself. Ángel García's lyrics reveal a myriad of forms, shadow, story, reflection, reverberation, negation, missive, reversal. If reading is a migration of thought across a page, these poems confound and renew our sense of direction. *Podemos decir poema-como-brújula, brújula-como-elegía, elegía-como-composición-de-ausencias*, which for García, consist of the endless shapes of a family's love translated across time and terrain, *lenguaje y linaje*, silence and song."

—Patrick Rosal, author of *The Last Thing: New & Selected Poems*

"*Indifferent Cities* scours time and space to recover and repair what borders, empire, violences, and intergenerational traumas attempt to erase and swallow: truth and origin. With skillful command across traditional and invented forms, as well as a multitude of valences, Ángel García gathers letters, archives, correspondence, oral histories, and his own lived experience to constellate a lineage that simultaneously askews fracture and redefines wholeness. From heartbreak to healvision, this collection gifts a framework to journey into the depths of ancestry to both probe and celebrate what is revealed. García knows, 'where I must go no directions exist.' These are poems chanting deep into a thousand ancestral moons, inhaling what has been forgotten and exhaling what will be a new collective future. *Indifferent Cities* reminds us, 'If there is no beginning, here is no end.' And in this way, this book asks each person to begin again, with every thread of history weaving us into the sunrise."

—Anthony Cody, author of *Borderland Apocrypha*

"*Indifferent Cities* is a heart-full book of seeking through the legacy of loss. And Ángel García leads the way with sobering delicacy, because the heart being entered is still at work with staying alive, is both his own and that of the 'living but lost' loved ones, is struggling under the fracturing estrangement of familial erasure, is set against a litany of distances that are at once old and growing wilder, growing unbearable, but for poetry— but for the surgical steadiness and staunching light of García's voice."

—Geffrey Davis, author of *One Wild Word Away*

WINNER OF THE INAUGURAL HELENA WHITEHILL BOOK AWARD

"To read *Indifferent Cities* is to linger in 'mud strewn' memory, ears pressed to the earth, listening to what courses underneath. As I read, I didn't realize I was holding my breath. What I was holding on to: my own lost languages, my own lost fathers. This book, put simply, bewildered me and broke me apart. As the poet writes: 'I try to remember what I've never known.' Verdant with visceral imagery and inventive form, *Indifferent Cities* seeks out ghosts: the ghosts of familial mythologies, the ghosts of displacement, the ghosts of language, of loneliness. From the very first poem, we feel the speaker's longing to know: 'my mother pours stove-warmed water over / my back to console me for what I can't understand.' I know that stove-warmed water intimately. In *Indifferent Cities*, we enter the vast arteries of the speaker's interiors. We zoom in so close, we can feel the aching jaw. From "Friday Night": 'for my father leaping up from the couch to grab him, if not / for my father smelling my brother's breath, their faces / so close I could have mistaken it for a kiss.' These poems are also formally and sonically felt—via grayscale (faint etchings), contrapuntals, and Spanish woven throughout. Poems tilt— literally—across the page: "[it began, the language slanting toward the bottom/corner of the page.]" From the poem 'Mourning':

<blockquote>

I kiss   my grandmother's cheek

a wet-slick gravestone   overgrown with dandelion

</blockquote>

Read across and down and with no map, the world of the living and the world of the dead intermingle, flush with lyrical tenderness. I love this book so much and I am honored to swim in its depths."

—*from the Judge's Citation by Jane Wong*

Ángel García, the proud son of Mexican immigrants, is the author of *Teeth Never Sleep* and currently teaches in the MFA Program at the University of Illinois at Urbana-Champaign.

Para mis antepasados, aquellos que conocí y aquellos que conoceré

I|N|D|I|F|F|E|R|E|N|T
C|I|T|I|E|S

Ángel García

Tupelo Press
North Adams, MA

Indifferent Cities
Copyright @ Ángel García

ISBN: 978-1-961209-32-9 (paper); 978-1-961209-50-3 (eBook)

Library of Congress Cataloging-in-Publication Data
Names: García, Ángel, 1981- author.
Title: Indifferent cities / Ángel García.
Description: First paperback edition. | North Adams, MA : Tupelo Press, 2025.
Identifiers: LCCN 2024054325 | ISBN 9781961209329 (paperback) 9781961209503 (eBook)
Subjects: LCGFT: Poetry.
Classification: LCC PS3607.A69 I53 2025 | DDC 811/.6--dc23/eng/20241125
LC record available at https://lccn.loc.gov/2024054325

Cover and text designed by Allison O'Keefe.
Cover image: Hand-painted postcard, "RECUERDO — Feliz año de 1911 — Narciso." Personal collection.
Courtesy of Ángel García.

First paperback edition: December 2025

All rights reserved. Other than brief excerpts for reviews and commentaries, no part of this book may be reproduced by any means without permission of the publisher. Please address requests for reprint permission or for course-adoption discounts to:

Tupelo Press
P.O. Box 1767
North Adams, Massachusetts 01247
(413) 664-9611 / Fax: (413) 664-9711
editor@tupelopress.org / www.tupelopress.org

Tupelo Press is an award-winning independent literary press that publishes fine fiction, non-fiction, and poetry in books that are a joy to hold as well as read. Tupelo Press is a registered 501(c)(3) non-profit organization, and we rely on public support to carry out our mission of publishing extraordinary work that may be outside the realm of the large commercial publishers. Financial donations are welcome and are tax deductible.

Table of Contents

Cenotes 1

ONE
Mexico City, 1985 5
Inhalar 6
Disinheritance 7
Leaving Home, 1986 8
Sin Nombre 9
On Visiting Mexico City, 2014 10
Topography 11
Progreso, 2023 12
Palíndromo 13
Yaxchilán, 2017 14
Leaving Home in Reverse, 1986 15
Brownsville, 1980 16
Cancún, 1978 20
Mexicali, 1952 21
Those Graves 22
Vestiges 29

TWO
Postales (1925) 33

THREE
A Child of Immigrants 49
Lessons in Unknowing 50
A Desire for Fluency 51
Burials 52
Mourning 54
Clave: in the Rhythm of Displacement 55
Places I've Learned to Forget 56
Haunted 57

Kindling	58
Water	62
Luto	63
Herencia	64
Rompecabezas	65
An Emptied House	66
Regret	67
Pastimes	68
Canto for my Love Language	70
Contenga la respiración	71
Diptych	72

FOUR

Mojado (1949)	75
Thirteen Years Old (1934)	76
Emancipación (Nov 1941)	77
Luna de Miel (Nov. 1941)	78
Telegram (Oct. 1942)	79
Covenant (Nov. 1942)	80
Pirámide de Hombres (1943)	81
Las Lavanderas (c. 1945)	82
La Bestia (1945)	83
Sin Zapatos (1948)	85
Thalassophobia (1952)	86
Deportation (1952)	87
3-Day Road Trip (1956)	88
Hotel Moreno (1959)	89
Thirteen Years Old (1961)	90
Asesinato (1963)	91
9-Day Road Trip (1964)	93
La Marea (1942-1964)	94

FIVE
Those Flowers … 97

SIX
The Road from My Mother's Womb … 105
Bautizo … 106
The River Coursing Through Us Is Dirty and Deep … 107
Before … 109
Detained … 112
Time Echoes Like Church Bells … 113
Dear Fake Father and Fake Mother, … 115
Nene … 116
Pesadilla … 117
Partial Interview … 118
In a Dream My Father Has a Stroke … 119
Visiting my grandmother's grave, I visit her house in a dream … 121
Cuéntame un cuento … 122
Layover / Overlay … 123
Secuestro … 125
[Memory] is a   space … 126
On a Good Day … 128
Exhalar … 129
Through the Snow … 130
Disculpa … 131
Guadalajara … 132

Hogar … 134

Notes … 137
Acknowledgments … 139
Gratitude … 141

Dead and dreaming exchange pities.
Huddled till dawn, in wooden echoing rooms,
they share their different and indifferent cities.

—Derek Walcott

Cenotes

lo que sé: un charco

lo que sé ahora: un estanque

lo que no sé y nunca sabré: un cenote

en cuyas aguas de sangre entro y chapoteo

                                        perdóname: mi intrusión

                                        perdóname: mi indiferencia

                                        perdóname: mi familia

                              por haberte abandonado al inframundo

en estas aguas la distancia entre nosotros crece

                no millas

            ni kilómetros

      pero a través

           de medidas desconocidas

                        todo era extraño   todo es extraño

                            una familia

                                convertido

                                    en extraños

tanto dolor por los vivos lejanos   tanto trauma

        se convierte en tradición

        arrastrándonos

      más adentro

                que estas frágiles traducciones nos acerquen

                      tanto como puedan

ONE

Todos aquí iremos desapareciendo
si nadie nos busca, si nadie nos nombra.

—Sara Uribe

Mexico City, 1985

Wave goodbye to your brothers, my mother tells me,
five-hundred feet in the air. Face pressed against
the cabin window, I wave. *There*, she points out. I
close my eyes tight and see them: on the sidewalk,
lined up in front of our house, waving back to me.

~

Years, later, my mother argues, *No, you didn't go, Rene went.*

I explain the memory. *You were just a baby.*

Maybe it was you, but how could you remember?

~

Still, I see them: oldest to youngest, tallest to shortest.
The three of them. Waving slow motion.

~

My first flight to Mexico, age four, this is my only memory:
triple-paned and blurred along the edges. I remember nothing else.
Not the destination. Not the arrival. Only, by default, the translation:
a blue sky turned white-lined horizon. Even my memories are imagined.

Inhalar

inhale: one last time the home you'll never know again

inhale: the country your father should have been for you

inhale: the phantom-ache of what was your endless hunger

inhale: your first earned dollar inside your palm

inhale: the language you'll learn against your will

inhale: the brine of wading in ocean water

inhale: mouths full of milk-white teeth

inhale: the family you'll lose by death or distance

inhale: the dead dogs piled along the highway

inhale: the last fire you made with your father

inhale: the house of obsidian daggers, the house of darkness

inhale: what will never be yours

inhale: this moment, an aleph

inhale: exhale

Disinheritance

there is no trace. no footprint to follow. nothing. I shut my eyes to imagine all of you.
  there were no traces. no footprints to follow. nothingness. I've shut my eyes and imagined you all.
from the dark I shape your face. From shadow, I manufacture memory.
  from the darkness I've shaped your faces. From shadows, I've manufactured memories.
I make an album of absence, hang a frame with no photograph along the corridor
  I've made an album of absences, hung frames with no photographs along the corridors
to your past—what a small word, past, to convey the century of my longing to know you.
  to your pasts—what a small word, pasts, to convey the centuries of my longing to know you all.
with only your name, a date, a birthplace, I try to remember what I've never known
  with only your names, dates, birthplaces, I've tried to remember what I've never known.

Leaving Home, 1986

from Plano, Texas to Torrance, California

We leave home and everything I know behind. I stare ahead toward what I cannot foresee. I ask—*Papi, what was your papi's name?* Through the fog we slow down. Time between ten and twelve tightens. My mother squeezes my hand as reprimand. I move from between them driver and passenger seat to my backseat. I wonder what I have done wrong. My mother reaches for his hand. His face brightens then blurs in the glow of oncoming lights. Watching him in the rearview mirror I vow to never again make my father cry.

Sin Nombre

I ask my father   *what is your mom's name?*

the wrinkles on his forehead clustered, his jaw pulsing tight

signal to me   *I've done something wrong.*

~

                                                                 I ask my brothers,
                                                                 who I burden
                                                            with remembering,
                                                     did I first meet her
                                                  when I was thirteen?

                                       Collectively, we compare memories.

                           She visited more often when we lived in Texas,
                                 they tell me, *but then we moved away.*

~

             Beside me, at my middle school promotion, she looks away from the camera.

~

In all the years before, I can't recall hearing her name,
not a phone call between my grandmother and my father,
him pushing me toward her for an uncomfortable embrace.
We went away and went even further, until she was someone
erased from memory: the next time I see her, she's already dead.

On Visiting Mexico City, 2014

A girl jumps rope
uno, dos, el lobo feroz
arms flailing as if on fire

A man sings for pesos
on the corner, his hand
swarmed by a song of bees

A woman meditates
cross-legged in a park
on the branch of a eucalyptus

In a country I only
know second-hand
I visit the museo de la antropología

I walk through
a church made of gold
once a mexica temple

I walk the zocalo
transformed into
a christmas wonderland

What I know
of the disappeared
the dead and the dreaming

are graffitied letters
being power-washed
from a government wall

Topography

I trace my finger along a worn map:

from Palenque to Tenosique
                        from Tenosique to Campeche
                                              from Campeche to Progreso

over jungle, through jungle, across
                        soft layers of wet soil, leaves
                                              outstretched for what remains

of the light beneath the canopy,
                        across warm-wet moss grown
                                            onto vines my grandmother cut

one hand blistered by the swing
                        of the machete, the other hand
                                            raw and bloodied by the reins

she pulled behind her: my near
                        dead grandfather on horseback,
                                            one child strapped to the saddle,

a newborn strapped across her
                        back, across four states, between
                                            now and the year 1945: the ten

fingers it takes to trace 800 kms,
                        two hands of distance to gather
                                            earth from every footpath we cross.

Progreso, 2023

In the cemeterio municipal,
          where [   ] might be buried
    I lose [   ] between the rows of graves.

          To not disturb the dead,
                   I text
            Where are [   ]?

Outside the church,
          where [   ] was baptized
              where [   ] married

[   ] sit
        beneath the shade
of a tropical almond, alone.

I'm tempted to run my hands
        along the church walls
but don't

        afraid of what
               I won't feel

        I've come with so much
              desire to find [   ]
meanwhile, I'm losing [   ].

Palíndromo

The machine breathing beside you exhales
like a prayer before bed. Night is a waiting
room of glass I run from before it shatters.

My apology, like my mourning, is belated:
I said goodbye years before you died. Now,
I walk the corridors of my grief with the lights

off. I can't miss someone I never knew: a lie
I tell to soothe my guilt. Still, you come to me
in my dreams. Your undying love, how it hurts.

*

How it hurts. In my dreams, your undying love:
you come to soothe me, to still my guilt. I can't
tell a lie. I miss someone I never knew. Off

the corridors of my grief, I walk with the lights.
Now, years before you died, I said goodbye.
My mourning is belated; my apology like

a room of glass before it shatters. I run from
a prayer. Night is like a waiting bed. Before
the machine exhales, I breathe beside you.

Yaxchilán, 2017

near the Usumacinta River

Off the footpath we were meant to follow

knee-deep in undergrowth, one tree trunk

indistinguishable from the next, no gauge

of direction inside the cacophony—howler

monkeys, bird calls—bellows and whistles

that echo through the never-ending expanse

...this is the deepest we've traveled. In time,

when the trees shift their weight, when leaf

shadows tremble into the graying sunset, we

trample again over our footsteps in the mud

and stop. It is this feeling—terrified to take

one more step in the wrong direction—I have

come for. I don't know where we are. In history,

I don't know why or how we belong—not yet.

Leaving Home in Reverse, 1986

from Torrance, California to Plano, Texas

To never again make my father cry   I disavow   his face
from the rearview mirror.   The glow of oncoming
lights   shrinks. His face darkens   then disappears.
My mother releases his hand.   From my backseat
where I wonder   what I've done wrong   I stand
to kneel between them   driver and passenger seat
My mother squeezes my hand as reprimand.   Time
between ten and twelve   loosens. Through the fog
we speed up.   I ask—*Papi, what was your papi's name?*
and stare ahead   toward what I can foresee.
We return home   to everything we've left behind.

Brownsville, 1980

When [   ] was kidnapped   up the block
                        my mother insisted   on more locks
        a deadbolt   barrel bolt   door chain   swing bar
                    wrought iron   over windows
                                        &
to leave   to   leave   to
        leave   to   leave
                    if   my father   loved   them

                                *

        Over late night coffee my parents whispered
                              (*always*)

    in the kitchen   —in different kitchens
   —inside different houses

                      —in different cities
to not wake my brothers asleep in the next room,

even though, of course, they were already awake.
From air ducts, from beneath bedroom doors,

from shadow-filled hallways, my brothers tried
to pull from our parents' mouths every word,

tried to gather them, like leaves, like twigs, like
kindling for the story my father would try to sell

my mother about a cousin on the other side who
wanted to cross, who wanted to come to this city.

                            *

This city　　　　　　　this house
　　　　　this kitchen　　　　　this table
　　　this coffee　　　　these words
this opportunity　　　　　　　this work
　　　　this money　　　　this life
this promise　　　　this country

　　　　　　　　　　*

When he was done, my mother protested. Pleaded.

She asked my father to reconsider.　　　Nothing

could be done. There was no stopping him. He knew

only one way to cross. Quickly, quietly, he left home.

　　　　　　　　　　*

　　　　　　In English or Spanish　　　they wouldn't listen

　　　　　　American or Mexican　　　they wouldn't listen

　　　　　　Legal or illegal　　　they wouldn't listen

　　　　　　Family or no family　　　they wouldn't listen

　　　　　　Wife or no wife　　　they wouldn't listen

　　　　　　Children or no children　　　they wouldn't listen

　　　　　　Lawyer or no lawyer　　　they wouldn't listen

　　　　　　Rights or no rights　　　they wouldn't listen

            Wetback, spic, or greaser   they wouldn't listen

                they didn't listen   they never listen

                          *

For days, then weeks:

      this dried out corpse

                    this desert

this river

          this current

                      this floating

this body swallowed

          this aching hunger

this the last time he kissed his wife and children goodbye

                        *

My mother insisted my brothers sleep in her bed.

(Afraid for my father who might never come home.
Afraid, too, of the men who might break in and take her children.)

Those nights she slept with a gun.

(The gun was always unloaded until my brothers fell asleep.
Late at night, she would load it ((slowly and quietly.))

Then, each morning she would unload it.

(One bullet for every man who would take one of her sons.
Should they be taken, another bullet for herself.)

Cancún, 1978

My brothers
                          flicker   the grainy sky

               burns they wave   8mm quick
       dubbed over   a   weeping song

                               fade to black

     my parents   jittered embrace
a newborn   the waves

    crescendo   then   quiet
before I was born   perches   on six plucked

strings   a gesture
    some future   I can   never join.

Mexicali, 1952

My mother boards a train with her family and leaves behind
everything she's known. Each of them wears only the clothes

on their backs, little else in tow, except the memory of a now
seventy-five-year-old woman trying to recollect the past. Her

father and mother sleep against each other in their seats while
all six children crowd the foot space between one row and the

next, quelled by the rhythm of tracks until they are each asleep.
Three days and two nights it takes them. One stop in Sonora,

her sister remembers, where they deboard and board another
train. Though she doesn't know it, this trip marks the beginning

of everyone she will lose. Her brother dead in twelve years. Her
mother dead in forty-nine. In between, every sibling wrapped

in the blankets of their own rancor until they no longer speak.
She peers outside the window. Inside it. Sees her father in its

reflection, just as years from now, she'll watch him from behind
a nursing home's glass window, longing to embrace him one last

time. He will die at nintety-nine though he wanted all his life to
live to one hundred years old. Rarely, from this place to another,

from one country to the next, are we afforded the solace we seek.
They left against her will, she says. And she has never been back.

THOSE GRAVES

It's a poet's simple duty to make pilgrimage. To lay
Flowers on the graves of other poets.
—John Murillo

Because of the way a name, any name,
is empty. And not empty. And almost enough.
—Larry Levis

From inside a shoebox beneath my grandmother's bed,
yellowed postcards, edges frayed, faded words her father
wrote her when she was a child.

To find you bisabuelo—a word I've only recently learned—I spend a summer, sweat-soaked in Yucatán searching through cemeteries. As my shadow lays over their gravestones, I pronounce the names of the dead: Salvador, Camilo, Margarito, Gumesindo.

Where others mourn their loved ones, I am merely a tourist.

I wander through row after dirt row with nothing
to offer: no flowers to lay at your grave, no sweet
bread, no liquor to sate your never-ending thirst.
Even as I kneel to wipe clean the names on the
loneliest gravestones, I know no prayer.

I've come emptyhanded, with so few words. Ancestry is a language I've not learned to speak.

At night, too tired to search for your grave, I imitate your cursive, its form and filigree, until it aches. Letter by letter, words echo from the page until my hand is no longer my own.

When I mean to write,
        I love you,
instead, I write
        I leave you.

By the time I learn your name, I can trace branches of lineage to loneliness. Most of what's been said in my life, I've needed translated. But not this. Bisabuelo—a word as soft as my grandmother's hands—is too tender a term for a stranger. I decide to call you by your name.

Name of the deceased: Narciso Palma Azueta

Date of birth: 9 de septiembre 1891
Date of death: 29 de mayo 1928

Place of death: Calle 36, casa 137, Progreso
Time of death: las quatro de la tarde

Cause of death: alcoholismo
Age of deceased: 36 años

Marital satus: divorciado
Children: Narciso, Deyanira, y Proserpina

I learn from family that you were a poet, though there are no poems left to be read. It's been said your last verses were etched onto your gravestone. No one knows where you are buried.

Long before your death, you leave behind everyone who loves you: your father and mother, your wife, your three children. Instead, you send postcards from ports and piers around the country. The words you wrote, a reminder of your absence. I imagine you selecting each postcard, unconcerned with the cost.

I don't know what I want more: to find your grave or to find your poems.

In 1911, you sent your mother a postcard to celebrate the new year. 103 letters. Twenty-three words. Two couplets I believe you wrote especially for her.

Creced y floreced, plantas hermosas
Creced y floreced y alzad al cielo

Esas ramas sonates y frondosas
Bañad en dulce lobreguiez el suelo

        Centered inside a purple-petaled iris, its once-green leaves and stems yellowed, is a portrait of you at twenty. No larger than a fingernail, your face faded by time

        and touch, I reach back. I read and reread your poem to translate it. Language, I imagine, will bring us closer.

        Beautiful flora, grow and bloom
        Grow and bloom, soar sky bound

        Those broadleaf branches that resound
        Bathe the ground in sweet gloom.

The cemetary itself, I learn, was moved decade ago. The dead, whose families paid dues, were moved: 206 bones congregated, in a deep and freshly dug grave.

But the dead whose names no longer echo: an ossuary. A shadow of spines, a knot of ribs, the stand of femurs & fibulas, tossed into a mass grave. Forgotten.

You came home only to die. It was weeks before someone found you, your stiff body decomposing in a hammock. It was not a pool of water, but bodily fluids and tequila that collected beneath you—the puddle so murky, there was no reflection to drown in.

But there are other versions:

You died on the beach not far from home, naked. Clothes laid out beside you like a carcass, your body floating face-up in a tidepool. Pupils coated mother-of-pearl; skin fluorescent in the moonlight. Details so precise, they could be part of a poem.

The poem, turns out, isn't yours. You didn't write it. It was written by a poet who died fifty-four years before you sent the postcard to your mother, a poet who wrote a continent away.

What we have between us is a distance that keeps expanding. The way a grandson might say, it's been twenty-four years since my grandmother passed—and say later—I've missed her for more than a millennia.

If on your gravestone your poem existed, it's gone unread for ninety-four years. I could not find it no matter where I looked. A poet once wrote, a name, any name, is almost enough.

It isn't, Narciso, it never will be.

Vestiges

Not the riverbank. Not the sedges
    or the black hum

of blow flies that feed off a corpse.
    Not the river. Not

its indifferent current. Not the bridge
    or how it bemoans

the loss of someone who's left town
    the year, the date,

unimportant. Not the address scribbled
    onto scrap paper.

Not the hospital or the room at home
    pulsing and humid.

Not the midwife who prays between
    parted legs. Not

the just born baby. Not his open mouth
    forming its first

word because the word is stillborn. Not
    the afterbirth,

its collapse, a memory of its last breath.
    No. None of this.

I pretend I'm well-mannered and polite.
    Wet with my grief.

Barefoot. Burdened by footprints I follow,
        those I've trekked

in the mud. I've come with no good sense
        of discretion. I seek

sins and secrets, what remains I excavate
        from the coffin

or confessional. For months I feed from
        my loneliness,

foaming at the mouth for what I'll never
        be given. To sate

myself, I excise, then pickle my tongue
        in a jar of ink.

TWO

Querida hija,i

A pesar de lo que diga tu madre, mi mejorl ve
decisión fue dejarte joven. Ahora, no necesitarásyou
distinguir entre quién recuerdas o quiénneed
imaginas que es tu padre.you
rememberyou
imagine you

Postales (1925)

Querida hija,

                                                            but

Tanto te extraño. Pero hay algunas cosas que no   i   can't
podemos cambiar. Para tu cuarto cumpleaños,   change
no pidas deseos que no se harán realidad. Rara   ,
vez lo hacen.   i   won't

Querida hija,

Sé que debes llorar a tu padre a pesar de que estoy vivo. El duelo es un fenómeno extraño: no mide qué tan lejos o cuánto tiempo me he ido.

your father
　　　　　　is

　　far
　　　gone.

Querida hija,

Compré un boleto de ida que me alejó de ti.
Compro las postales y pago los gastos de envío
para traerme de vuelta a ti, sin importar el costo.

                                        i
                                    ought
                                        to
                                            s
                                        ay
                                            ,
                                    regardless

Querida hija,

                                                                my   vice: death
Mi consejo: elige la muerte antes de que te elija a   i choose
ti. Pronto moriré y será la única decisión que   it
tome sin arrepentirme.

Querida hija,

Quizás nada de esto tenga sentido para ti: por qué elegí el lenguaje en lugar de estar contigo. No tengo respuestas Antes de morir, mi última comida será mi lengua.

                                            is

                              language

                    a

                    tongue

Querida hija,

Mis palabras se balancean en una sola línea: single line   a
cuervos acicalando sus plumas negras.   f

Querida hija,

Sin duda, tu familia me ha comparado con la marea, que entra y sale de tu vida. Pero si me quedara, verías que soy una corriente de resaca.

         doubt
           a   tide,
flowing into
  our life.   i
                  am a rip
current.

Querida hija,

No caben todas las palabras que he querido
decirte en esta postal. Este es uno de mis
muchos lamentos constantes. Siempre seré tu primero.　　of my　　constant
　　　　　　　　　　　　　　　　　　　　　　　　　　　　　　regret

Querida hija,   a

Que tonta te sentirás en el futuro, cada vez que   future
pases por una cantina y escuches trinar las
botellas, creyendo que estoy ahí, adentro.   lie
                                                     there, inside

Querida hija,

Algunos padres se quedan, algunos padres se van. Ya no nos pertenecemos. Ahora eres la hija de otro hombre. ¿Qué quieres de mí que no te hayan dado ya?

                          long
     ng   you
are   the
daughter

Querida hija,

Incluso en los trozos de papel más pequeños, he tratado de escribir la historia de mi vida. Si soy indigno de la memoria, todavía no quiero ser olvidado.

                      the

                              life story   i

                   m unworthy of

Querida hija,

Perdóname por favor. Ruega a tus abuelos que me perdonen. Como niño y como padre, les he fallado a todos. Todo lo que escribo, leído o no leído, espero que me libere.

                                                              lea   ve me.

                                                                     unread

THREE

But perhaps a person only has two real residences:
the childhood home and the grave.

—Valeria Luiseli

A Child of Immigrants

The phone rings. I pick up. The voice, unrecognizable. Distant words. Between, I hear my mother's name. I cover the mouthpiece and call out for her to pick up. From somewhere else, she answers the line. Yells from another room, *okay, hang up*. Only, I don't. In a language I know will never be mine she speaks to someone in a country I will never know. Still, I listen. I coil the cord around my finger, fist, and wrist. Long after she says goodbye and hangs up, my body still marked by what I don't understand.

Lessons in Unknowing

shhh   eres muy joven para saber eso

                         shshhh   no hables del pasado

[a hand squeeze]

                 no puedo recordar   shhh

                                fue hace mucho tiempo

[a nudge of the elbow]

                         tú no tienes que saber de eso

         no quiero recorder ese tiempo   shhh

                         shhh

[a hand placed on the thigh]

                         [a kick under the table]

                                    [a stare two seconds too long]

             no quieres saber, recordar

es de mala educación hacer tantas preguntas

                               no preguntes sobre lo que no sabes

A Desire for Fluency

Plano, Texas

I beg my mother, tear-filled, beside her bed,
    I want to talk Mexican.

In the bathroom, applying eyeliner, she responds,
    Spanish, mi'jo, not Mexican.

Burials

We weigh in our hands what little we own to decide what we'll leave behind:

    a micro machine   *hot wheels*   *slammers and pogs*   *duplicate comic cards of our least*

    favorite marvel heroes   *a second-hand gi joe action figure*   *a wallet-sized school photo*

In the dark, flashlights in hand, uncertain we have much vision to offer, we write in our finest handwriting one letter each to our future selves.

        dear angel,   *dear rene,*

All night we listen to June Bugs skitter across the ceiling, afraid they might fall into our mouths.

~

Our parents already at work, we fix bowls of Corn Flakes with too many spoons of sugar. We watch summer reruns in our underwear. When the heat dies down, we arrange our belongings, together with our letters, inside an empty cigar box and step outside.

In the backyard, shovels in hand, we dig in tandem. On our knees, we bury the box and push the mounds of dirt back over it.

Because we know what lies ahead—the cardboard boxes stacked beneath our beds—we walk heel toe, heel toe from the hole we've just dug to our front door. One time, two times for good measure to trace on paper the promise we make to return.

~

One summer to the next: a new city, a new house, a new school with no friends. We sit together in a cafeteria and make do with the familiar: the fresh scent of pine-mopped floors, the still-wet lunch tables wiped clean with bleach, the aroma of once-frozen food now warming in their trays.

Other days, we never make it. On our walk to school, my brother and I begin to cry. Wet-faced, we convince ourselves to run back home, our backpacks flapping behind us. There, in her room, we kiss and hug and beg our mother to let us stay home; for her to stay home with us. Today, just today, please, one day when what me mean is forever.

Mourning

I kiss	my grandmother's cheek
a wet-slick gravestone	overgrown with dandelion
my love hoarded	inside a cheap coffin
the bodies, white-speckled	trembling in unison
like a prayer:	a crow's beak pecking
something soft in an evergreen	junipers shaking off the last season
needles piled on the ground	a halo

Clave: in the Rhythm of Displacement

I come home
we're leaving
no llores

pack up
hurry
mi'jo

tidy up
mop the floors
leave the fridge

your room
spotless
unplugged

pack your things
bag your clothes
what we leave

quickly
right now
gets left

despedir
tell your friends
you start school

adios
goodbye
next week

we are here
fold up those
we are home

unpack
boxes
for now

Places I've Learned to Forget

3601 Wildwood Pl.
Plano, TX 75074 } Kindergarten Roundup, Pre-school

Meyler Elementary School, 1st Grade { 1158 W. 226th St. Torrance CA 90502

Eshelman Avenue Elementary School, 2nd Grade { 25615 Oak St. Lomita, CA 90717

212 E Commonwealth Ave.
Alhambra, CA 91801 } Granada Elementary School, 3rd – 4th Grade

124 N. Fourth St.
Alhambra, CA 91801 } Garfield Elementary School, 5th Grade

4423 Barrett Ave.
Los Angeles, CA 90032 } Garfield Elementary School, 6th Grade

836 N. Olive Ave.
Alhambra, CA 91801 } Garfield Elementary School, 7th – 8th Grade

10 N. Primrose Apt C
Alhambra, CA 91801 } Alhambra High School, 9th Grade

Narbonne High School, 10th Grade { 1158 W. 226th St. Torrance CA 90502

Millikan High School, 10th – 12th Grade { 3436 Palo Verde Ave. Long Beach, CA 90808

HAUNTED

My grandfather moved from place to place every time he'd see a ghost—others were inescapable. For 99 years he refused to say a single word about his father—who he was or wasn't—to no one. Nearly a century, and not one word. I've never seen a ghost. Still, I know what it means to be cursed. God willing, I won't live as long a life as my grandfather. My ghosts come for me every night. Others, I continue to resurrect. I need only live long enough to bury each one—I refuse to die possessed.

Kindling

When your father wanders deeper into the fields,
pitchfork in hand, he fades slowly into silhouette.

What you cannot see, you strain to hear beyond
the crackle and spit of the bonfire you sit beside:

each of his footsteps rustling through desert tea,
each scrape of every tine when they pierce soil.

The fire begins to wane, as it does. Without fail,
the dark encroaches. What you cannot fathom,

in the embers of waiting for your father to return
is how they'll burn from this day forward, always,

or how smoke, the scent of it, will forever obscure
time. Long before the fields you sit in cease to be:

red sand verbena and cheatgrass, the rib-thin cows
and their starving calves, what your father brings

back on his pitchfork is lost somewhere between
what you remember and what you imagine when

he smothers one, sometimes two tumbleweeds on
top of the fire. Through the billow of smoke, you

hear stems snap, and then, watch as seed pods
blaze into a whirlwind of reddened starlight, watch

them float and fade into the black sky, the color
a father fades into in this story while fireside a boy

waits for his father to gather kindling from a field
—only, it's me. I was the boy, not you. Through

the smoke that drifted, further and closer, between
us I watched my father's face: his incandescent eyes,

his cheeks soot-smeared, a thin grin inch along his
lips...how else can I say it, except to say my father

became a boy again, and sitting across from me, he
was someone I could not recognize. The boy my

father once was, was a stranger. I didn't need him
to remind me that he loved me, then, because he

said it often: in our backyard back home, the two
of us seated on the living room sofa, during hours-

long trips we took, tumbleweed stumbling across
the roads that brought us here. I watched him, that

night, tend to the fire that kept us warm all through
the night into the early hours of the morning, how

he seemed to know exactly what it needed, when it
needed it: more kindling, another piece of wood,

blowing on the embers to make them breathe. I
admit, I was jealous of fire. What I could not have

said then, and what I'm certain of now, is that what
we shared between us in the quiet, was mostly quiet,

when all I wanted was older than fire itself: the stories
my father never told of who he was and where we

came from, stories I feared, he was unable, or worse,
unwilling to tell. Memory is not a complaint, but even

then, just a little boy, silence was something I did
not want to inherit, or pass down to my son, should

I one day have one, because I don't want you to live
with a fervent ache of knowing so little about the man

you love. I want you, instead, to hear the stories from
me: not in a letter, not in a poem, not from the small

crowd of mourners at a wake who'll whisper about
the man your father once was, the man you will one

day, God forbid, mourn forever as a stranger. I want
you to hear the stories from me, while we sit across

the shadows of a fire we've made, smoke lingering on
both our bodies, contented to sleep beside each other

long after the fire has burned off and the morning has
grown cold because you know not only how to tend

a fire, but how to stoke it with story. Maybe one day,
when you are the age I was, I'll say the word tumble-

weed, and you'll see my father emerge from the dark
to tend the fire we will sit beside. I'll tell you, in that

moment, how afraid I was, with so little to say between
us, of one day losing my father. I'll remind you, what

my father gave us was all he was able to give, kindling,
fire, the ache that will linger in us always, like smoke.

WATER

herself a child she was left to watch
over six children who were not her
children but her mother's children

how quickly she became a mother
when they no longer called her by her
name and began to call her mama

how it must hurt all these years later
to lose both her daughters and sisters
in rivers between them. Wider. Deeper.

Luto

there at the altar
she rests her head

god is candlelight
a flame flickering

a confession to her father
between her palms *te perdono por abandonarme*

~ ~

inside her she looks out
a dark room through rain-streaked windows

she hears in an empty house
her sons hung from a wall

and prays her rosary
perdoname *quiero desaparecer*

Herencia

You never mentioned the switches or stones, the unhung crucifijo
tearing into your back, your father running you out, *no eres mi hijo*.

Late-night, TV aglow, you never said the name of who hurt you.
Instead, my head cradled in your lap, you'd tell me, *I love you mi'jo*.

What bones we may break, may we break the bones of our pasts,
skeletons dragged over scarred lifetimes, *en nombre del padre, el hijo*

the ghosts of our wounds, dark-winged words we've never shared,
are what keep us bound, rooted for generations, *de tal palo tal astilla*.

You've never been your father, just as I won't be you. Still, how
could I be a better father, Papi, when I've never been a good son.

Rompecabezas

We spread the pieces across her dining room table and leave
enough space for where, most days, she'll eat her meals alone.

We search for each corner and every edge to form a frame—
the other pieces, the hundreds, we group into piles by color:

we crimson, we auburn, we ochre and amber. We assemble:
knobs to their pockets, loops to their slots, bumps to sockets.

We rise and sit and circle while time slips away. The last few
pieces, we place together side by side without a word between

us, my Spanish poorer than her English: a fall landscape in this
country somewhere so far from what we know it's unfamiliar.

An Emptied House

Carpets shampooed into
near-perfect triangles.

Fridge unplugged, the door
wide open. Its insides dark
and immaculately empty.

Family photos unhung
from the walls and still

their frames remain.
Each caulked nail hole
raised slightly like a scar.

Beneath the sink, etched
into the paint, an imprint

of every cleaning bottle.
A desiccated washcloth
hung over the trap. Upside

down a hatch of houseflies
dead on the windowsill.

Regret

My grandmother and I watch *Little House on the Prairie*. Today, Mrs. Wilder assigns Laura and the other schoolchildren family trees due at the end of the month: *with names, dates, and relationships*. Albert, we know, has no family. So, when the other children sprint home afterschool to ask their parents where they come from, Albert goes fishing with a friend instead. At the river, while they hook bait, Simon says Albert will have an easy time with the assignment because, *you know, you're a bastard and all*. Albert, fuming, lunges at Simon and complains how he doesn't like that word. Over the break, Larry H. Parker parades his clients in a montage of the injured and uninsured. To convince us how hard he'll fight, he yells each promise, spittle stuck in the creases of his thin lips, until his most successful client touts his 2.1-million-dollar settlement. The next day, Nellie finds Laura and Albert eating their lunch beside the school and sees an opportunity. She says to them both *Albert couldn't make a family tree if he wanted to* and to add insult to injury, throws a branch on his lap and quips, *this is about as much family tree as you've got*, before she saunters back to Oleson's Mercantile. An elderly woman who's fallen on the floor claims Life Alert technology is life-saving. To Mr. and Mrs. Ingalls surprise they find out Albert has a father. Only, he doesn't seem too interested in having a son; instead, he wants a farmhand. A voiceover promises a well-paid, rewarding career in underwater diving and welding and a 1-800 number swipes across the screen. Albert, in the end, can stay with the Ingalls family. His biological father decides Albert would be happier with his new family. We don't speak, my grandmother and I, over the forty-eight-minute episode. Next week, there'll be another happy ending.

Pastimes

for my brother Rene

Bored with staring out our windows, bored with out-of-state plates, bored with punch bug, bored by our thirst and nagging hunger, bored by *La Bamba* playing on repeat, by our mother singing off-key from the front seat while she stretched her legs over the dashboard, bored by watching the rosary hung from the rearview mirror sway in incessant circles, wondering if little Jesus felt as sick as I did when I read in the back of the van, we'd begin—my brother and I—to identify changes from one weekend to the next: white crosses mourning a life lost erected along the highway, half a hillside of corn harvested by faceless men in straw hats, the slow fade of sun burnt billboards peddling Mexican beer or the beach-side resort, or entire hillsides leveled and framed with towers of wrought iron, one story after another raised for the spectacular views no one could afford to admire from the first floor to the rooftop terrace as every apartment went unsold and sat empty for years, or the highway itself, laid and laid again over the fault lines that shifted beneath it, roadside signs that warned us to slow down, to merge lanes, warned us of dangerous turns ahead, warned of rocks falling from the cliff's edge, or the roadside flares that surrounded a two-car pile-up, or the squad car spotlights that shone on a car crashed into the median, shone over the bodies flung from the car as we passed in slow motion, our faces pressed against the window clouded bored by where we'd been and bored by where we'd never get to.

Bored by where we'd been and bored by where we'd never get to, our breath swelling and shrinking on the windowpanes, our faces side by side as we sat on the bench seat gazing out the back windows, we began calling out the animals we saw along the way, the emaciated horses grazing in a sun-filled field or the earth-colored cows being corralled into their pen, until one of us began to narrate the animals that followed behind us, gaining: a cheetah that sprinted across the plateau so quickly its paws barely touched the ground, or a tiger that jumped in bounds, its muscles pulsing between its stripes, or a falcon that flew over the hillsides, its shadow undulating between and over the spring green wild grasses, its feathers trembling with speed, until the animals caught up and ran beside us, propelled purely by the pleasure of our imagination, faster, stronger, possible only in our minds until we could see not one, but many, racing along the kilometer markers and lane reflectors, animals that would arrive home long before we did, to the place we longed to be: on the bottom bunk of our bed, opening the tub of margarine we kept beside a book of fantasy, the one book we owned and read nightly, brother to brother, until one of us fell asleep—and from the tub we pulled our best pill bug and placed them on a sheet of construction paper, ushered them along the track we had drawn, betting only pennies, as they raced toward the finish line, toward the direction of one day when we would no longer be here, not knowing we'd lose each other in the distance, when we could no longer pass the time together.

Canto for my Love Language

I have suffered a lot because of your absence
you don't even feel sorry for leaving me
when I'm in your arms

you carry a wound in your chest
they say that at night
I am your silence and your time

I'm afraid of losing you losing you later
love me again come back my love
Come and calm my anxieties

to love you is to conjugate the verb
to love in solitude

Contenga la respiración

hold your breath: your parents ~~will die~~ are dead
hold your breath: when men flash you their dark dicks
hold your breath: your brother's been runover by a semi
hold your breath: nadie te quiere en este casa
hold your breath: a kid kidnapped from up the block
hold your breath: tu no eres mi hijo
hold your breath: your father has been arrested
hold your breath: switchblade give-me-your-cash-quick
hold your breath: again, your [   ] is in the hospital
hold your breath: a piss-wet dollar placed in your palm
hold your breath: as the belt rips into your thigh
hold your breath: tu no eres mi hija
hold your breath: for one day, someday, when the pain subsides
hold your breath: until you're brown in the face

Diptych

Slowly,   the dark. I am   a boy.
      Arms outstretched, I measure   time
fingers graze each family photo
                      I loved them

    until I stand in the doorframe   I was kept
      Outside   Kept away. Kept at a distance.
  through an open window. Slivers of
moonlight melt into the room.   they never
                 belonged to me.

      beside the bed.   I've told you too much.
  time   now

       inescapable
               there may be

Watching them, I begin to weep.   love in that dark.
    why.   Tell me,

               you   will disappear

FOUR

Mojado (1949)

"go before him unto..."

he walks toward the water he walks toward water with little faith afraid he walks into the water he sinks in the water beneath the water he crosses himself under water he crosses   to the other side

Most boats have cast off into the Gulf taking the men whose skin smell like the sea. Barefoot on the beach, only the wind whistling through their hair, the girls tiptoe across the seaweed-covered shore unbothered. They approach the berthed boat on the beach, *la surgida*, to ask the old man who sands its hull if he would take their photo. Just turned thirteen, Proserpina stands between two girlfriends in a sleeveless floral dress—hand-made by her mother—head bowed, squinting, her thin lips etched into a smile, a mother-of-pearl beret clip keeping the hair from her face. Borrowed from her stepfather, the camera catches her dress tucked and tied between her knees from when she alone waded hip-deep into the water, the other girls only watching from a distance, knowing Proserpina's mother had asked them to stay away from the beach and to not step foot into the water, unescorted. Eyes closed and alone in the water, before the boats will return with men whose bodies are turned white with salt, she imagines she will live her entire life on the peninsula. Holding tightly the hands of her girlfriends—all of them years from becoming women—they cannot not yet fathom the reasons why they should fear men.

Thirteen Years Old (1934)

Proserpina en la playa de Progreso

Emancipación (Nov 1941)

from Progreso, Yucatán to Guadalajara, Jalisco

In 1941 my grandmother boards a ship to join a man she's been forced to marry. She takes with her, what little she owns: family photos, postcards her father sent her before he died, a marriage license placed carefully above ill-fitting dresses, seven letters wedged between her and her good name. Proserpina E-s-t-r-a-d-a Palma.

From the ship to a train, from one train to another, she loses count of how many stops and how many states she crosses. Over the constant clack of the tracks, she mulls over *embarked* or *banished*, trying to decide which word she'll choose for the life story she'll write fifty-seven years later. Twelve pages in a spiral bound notebook no one will read until she is dead.

On the platform, she waits for a man she will hardly recognize. Todo era extraño, she says, her voice scribbled from the end of a ball-point pen. Yes. Everything is strange still. I watch her waiting, suitcase in hand, and I fear for her future. What I wish for her is an alternate ending, one I know does not exist.

Luna de Miel (Nov. 1941)

Guadalajara, Jalisco

She arrives midmorning. When she disembarks, she spots him through the throng of shoulders, relieved. But when he approaches, arms raised, she clutches her dress. After their embrace, he asks, *Ready to go home?* She feels the sand beneath *Todo era extraño.* her bare feet, hears the ocean, can make out the beacon of the lighthouse in the distance until he grabs her hand and pulls her through the train station.

They arrive to a single room in a stranger's house. A small bed beneath a smaller window. A lone chair in the corner. He insists they go out for dinner. *To celebrate*, he urges, *our marriage*. But when he buys her a drink, she declines. No…thank you. On their walk home, she lingers. She drags every footstep *No puedo confiar en lo que no conozco* deliberately. Time feels two shoe sizes too tight; it aches.

After she bathes, she slowly opens the bedroom door. She watches the light cut across his body. She studies his chest, each deep breath to determine if he's awake or asleep. Asleep, she decides, she closes the door behind her. She sits in the chair, in the darkest corner in the room, and dreams of being back on the train, homebound. *No recuerdo cómo llegué a su cama.* She wakes up sobbing.

He hit me. I had the baby in my arms and couldn't defend myself. I've left him and taken the baby with me. I'll be in the City waiting. I want to come back home to Yucatán. Please let me return.

Telegram (Oct. 1942)

Ciudad de Mexico

Go back to your husband. He told us he's sorry for what he's done. You're married. You should be with your husband. Your son needs his father. Go back. He told us he regrets what he's done. Go. When you're back where you belong, he said he'll apologize. Your home is with your husband. He, and your son, are the only family you have now.

Covenant (Nov. 1942)

On centuries of stone, seventeen men seated in four rows pose for photos they'll later send home to their families: wives and children, siblings, parents: un recuerdo de Uxmal. After clearing for months what the machines left behind, the bulldozers and cranes long-gone, the men have traded in the saws and axes, machetes, short-handled hoes, and dressed in their best: newsboys, fishermen caps, fedoras and straw sombreros; buttoned shirts fresh pressed; high-waisted trousers creased and cuffed; wing-tips, romeos, two tones, and boots gleaming from their last shine. Juan sits (third row, far left), his hair parted off-center, his fingers interlaced, twenty years old, the youngest among them. The foreman collects from each of them a few pesos to pay a native boy who'll guide them through the site where he'll wait for them to pose—chins, backs, and shoulders straight—to take their photos before El Palacio del Gobernador, El Pirámide del Hechicero, El Cuadrángulo de las Monjas, and the ball court where he'll explain the short-lived lives of men who sacrificed themselves. Juan will send home to his wife, their two children, a letter written by lamp light stating that he will be home soon, that he is fine, that he is holding things together—a lie he'll enclose with photos but no money and send off by mail in the morning while his wife gets up to breastfeed their daughter without the slightest idea, for months, where her husband has been.

Pirámide de Hombres (1943)

Juan en las ruínas de Uxmal

Knee deep at the river's edge, half dressed, a row of women wash: blouses, slips, one woman's worn dress pressed so firmly between fists and river stone, her knuckles bleed. In a nearby clearing, their children chase one another beneath their mother's sunset shadows. Feet firmly on the bank, my grandmother stands guard. What lies ready, waiting always, to snatch an unattended child into the jungle or drag one beneath the current, is insatiable. Patient. Over the cacophony of jungle, each roar, every howl, the incessant chirping, she can still hear the wail of the last woman to lose her child. Each night, she pleads to leave this place. Begs even. The only silence she hears, she hears from her husband and God.

Las lavanderas, (c. 1945)

after Lola Álvarez Bravo

La Bestia (1945)

from Palenque, Chiapas to Tenosique, Tabasco

he clears the jungle for track
                                    in Palenque
                                                                                  she washes clothes on river rock

the low growl of the tractor
                                    trembling
                                                                                  near the river's edge she sweats

fever spreads through his body
                                    heart tense
                                                                                    from her fear of the tree lines

he cuts the motor and stumbles
                                    back home
                                                                                   she tells her child to stay close

everything green grows into dark
                                    shadows
                                                                                   begin to stalk their young prey

what slowly feeds on his wrought body
                                    will kill
                                                                                  a child momentarily unattended

dragging his body through a trail
                                    his cries
                                                                                   echoed by a mother who mourns

for home, he wants to go back home
                                    to live
                                                                                   she knows they must leave here

to get away from the train, the beast
                           la bestia
                                        that will consume her family whole

He was born with no shoes. Breastfed with no shoes. Took his first bath with no shoes. When he began to crawl, he had no shoes. When he took his first steps, he had no shoes. *No shoes*, were his first words. And at night, as he listened to the cascade of waterfalls, he had no shoes. He slept with no shoes.

He dreamt that night and every night with no shoes. As the sun rose, he had no shoes. He was lonely with no shoes. He was hungry with no shoes. When his brother was born and he fed him what little he had to eat, he had no shoes. When he began to work, he cut sugarcane with no shoes.

When his father told him he was not his son, he had no shoes. When his father ran him from their home, and he ran through the jungle, he had no shoes. When he hid in the trees, he had no shoes. When he heard his mother calling, he had no shoes. On his first day of school, he had no shoes. He didn't think twice about it until another student asked him, *why are you barefoot?* The next day and every day after, he felt ashamed with no shoes.

Sin Zapatos (1948)

Ciudad Vallez, San Luis Potosi

Thalassophobia (1952)

from Guadalajara, Jalisco to Cuyutlán, Colima

Because his children have never seen the ocean he borrows a tent and drives them away, three hours to the coast. On the beach, he sets up camp for his family of six. Overnight, the tide rises and floods them out. Beneath the moonlight, he shakes them awake and tells them to run. *Your grandfather,* my mother says, *had thrown me into the water earlier that day. He didn't know how afraid I was of the ocean.* All that night, as they sleep, she lays awake, trembling. She alone watches the water rise inside the tent. She tries to scream but nothing comes out.

Deportation (1952)

from *to*

[

]

3-Day Road Trip (1956)

from Brownsville, Texas to Chicago, Illinois

In a 1951 Bonita Blue Metallic four door Lincoln Cosmopolitan my father drives his family away. He is only fifteen, without a license and without his citizenship.

Two days before they depart, he struggles to drive manual. His little brother begs to get behind the wheel. But for $500 dollars, he knows better. This is all they've got.

In Missouri, sleep deprived, he nearly backs into a creek and blows a tire. There is no spare in the trunk. He must decide: take them or leave them in the car. It is 1:07am.

Because they are hungry, his mother tells him to pull over at a diner. *No n*ggers, no Mexicans*, a sign reads in the window. Some hunger needs no translation.

Knowing no one will pick up a Mexican hitchhiker, he tells them, *Lock the doors. Stay in the car.* He walks into the darkness not knowing what he'll have to pay.

When they arrive to his brother's apartment, his brother slams the door in their faces. They are not welcome here. While his siblings sleep, his mother decides to go back.

He tries to sleep streetside but can't. It's too loud and bright a city. In two days, he'll drive his two sisters and younger brother back home to their father.

He leaves his mother to find a place to live. A basement apartment in Pilsen where they'll stay. Still uncertain about his future, he tells her, *I'll be back, god willing.*

I watch my mother sort linens from a still warm basket two-hundred and twenty-seven miles from where she'd first learned, only eleven-years-old, to fold hotel towels, pillowcases, and sheets, the soft geometries of domestic labor. *Room 16*, she says, *is where it was stolen*—a story I'd heard before: some pesos missing from a dresser drawer, a gold necklace with a gold virgin lifted from a nightstand. *Eventually, we all got accused of stealing something*, she tells me. Back home, I help my mother spread over the bed fresh sheets, watch her crease them with the back of her hand into precise folds beneath the pillows, pile hand and bath towels on the bed corner, habits kept from a country ago: to do what was expected and do it well, beyond suspicion. *Even when you have nothing, someone will want to take it from you*, she says, describing how the white paisley of the red carpet blurred beneath her shoes as she sped down the corridor— first away from, then back toward the room where it first happened, now empty—to pick up her yellow underwear, ripped, the elastic broken, crumpled and left in the corner.

HOTEL MORENO (1959)

Mexicali, Baja California

Told days ago   she'd need
new photos   she resigns
to go   but despite   his best
soft talk   *dame una sonrisa* she
bows her head   and frowns

     —flashclick—

She raises her brow   when he
insists   *sonriete mi'ja* a
glare she's learned   to
give   men who get
     too familiar

     —flashclick—

Una sonrisa   *linda*
   como tu nombre   still
she refuses   to smile for a
country   she does not
      want

     —flashclick—

She scowls when he says
Vas a tener   *una vida nueva*
tired of the false promises
she's refused
      to swallow

     —flashclick—

THIRTEEN YEARS OLD (1961)

Fotos por una visa

Asesinato (1963)

Los Angeles, California

From a	back seat	in the	last row
of a	classroom	lights off	blinds closed
a man	speaks from	his desk	on film
his words	incomprehensible	dust dancing	past the
projector lens	cuba	panama	mexico
peru	the few	words she	understands
while somewhere	from an	island over	the pacific
the sky	flashes white	then red	and green
hydrogen particles	re-entering	the earth's	atmosphere
in a	dazzling	display	and today
as she	has since	the day	she arrived
refuses	to speak	English	though all
her teachers	insist	*English only*	*No Spanish*
Nearly	a year	later *Nov.*	*22nd 1963*
the lights	flipped on	my mother	watches her
teacher *Mis.*	*Yon-son*	crumble into	her chair
somewhere	behind her	and to	her right

                weeping   she asks   *¿qué pasó?*   everyone now

from the   front row   to the   back row

                weeping   *wat*   *hapen*   she asks

unaware   ignored   until someone   translates

for her   *mataron*   *el*   *yay-ef-que*

9-Day Road Trip (1964)

from Los Angeles, California to Progreso, Yucatán

Between the squealing brakes in stop and go traffic she hears *4037 kilómetros mas.*

~

Just now the hot, tar-bottomed feet of her younger sister stretching across her lap.

~

Her cheek pressed against the glass. She yawns. Her breath condenses into fumes.

~

A car horn sounds then fades. Startled, she wakes as a pitch-black two-lane highway.

~

The distinct odor of ten bodies sweating bumper to bumper inside a station wagon.

~

When another sister tosses in her makeshift bed she almost swerves into the fast lane.

~

Her braid winds tightly around her perspiring neck, resembling a radiator hose on the road.

~

One day away from Progreso, a telegram arrives before them that declares her brother dead.

~

On their return, through the highway, she sees him in the distance. His mirage undulating.

La Marea (1942–1964)

por mi tío

Death came for my uncle when he was only a newborn
—then changed its mind: pulled his body from between
his parents as they slept in bed, cradled him in both its
arms and carried him away. But stopped. *What* changed,
no one knows—only his wails woke his parents. They found
him on the floor near the front door, cracked open—his blue
cold body sodden with morning dew. It took them all day
to bring him back.
                      But twenty-two years later death came
again: saw my uncle, eyes closed, in a bed of water and pulled
him under. Though now's not the time to say it: from his death
my grandparents bought their first house in this country. From
tragedy came a new fortune without which we'd all be drowning.

FIVE

Those Flowers

- *Follow the sources.*

I search through hundreds of documents: birth certificates: baptismal records: marriage licenses: church records: death certificates: to find who you are: who we are: where we are: where we've been: where we've come from: what we've come through:

- *What sources can you trust?*

I hunch over the good light:
                        squint & distance documents
                                            :days: months: years: decipher
details: I don't know I can trust:
                        19th century script: colloquialisms
                                            :regional procedure: 1851 or 1857:
a or an *o*: your name misspelled:
                      procerpina: proserpina: the one:
                                        I mourn. the other: I remember:

- *What is your relationship to this research?*

                        I struggle to understand
                                            :how history speaks
days: months: years:
                    of strangers: stranger places:

                                              :their names in my mouth like foil

- *What gaps exist? What silences?*

[no results found]   [400 Bad Request]   [no entries found]

[503 Service Unavailable]   [refine search]   [502 Bad Gate-way]

- *What variables have you not considered?*

> Los documentos que busca: son demasiado viejos: nuestros archivos solo datan a 1920: si desea acceder a esos documentos: deberá ir al archivo [   ]: en la cuidad: [   ]: estás en el lugar equivocado

- *What is your relationship to this research?*

   you: alive: the early morning haloing: from one side: to the other: until we: meet: in light:

- *What gaps exist? What silences?*

Twenty years after your passing: I read you:

:inside a repurposed 5 subject:

spiral bound notebook:

:I can't be certain the year

[xxxxxxxxxxxx]:

:[xxxxxxxxxxxx]

you put pen to paper: *La historia de mi Vida de Proserpina Palma de Estrada* :how long it took to handwrite:

an entire lifetime:

:inside 11in x 8½in

struggled print:

scrawled:

blue ink, black ink

:41 college-ruled pages

- *What sources can contribute?*

every photograph: of you: I find: I collect it: sort it: match it: to place: match to year: a page number: peer through the loop: to decipher: I stare: into: your eyes: so long: you begin to fade: into the stacks of photos: *you:* and *you:* and *you:* and *you:* the myriad versions: of meaning: repeated until meaning: is lost: abuelita: abuelita: abuelita: abuelita: so many: possibilities: left behind:

- *What sources can contribute?*

    artifacts: possible: postcards: possible: ticket stubs: possible: wedding cake: possible: automobiles: possible: lies: possible: metaphor: possible: albums: possible: lyrics: possible: letters: possible: song titles: possible: names: possible: parents: possible: prayer cards: possible: translations: possible: a crucifix: possible: a map: possible: a name: possible: a child: possible: a gift: possible: a two-dollar bill: possible: a recipe card: possible: a carrot cake: possible: a love: possible: a life: possible: a love story: possible: alive: possible: a love: possible: regret: possible: a denial: possible: a confession:

- *What gaps exist? What silences?*

> how much do your remember: how much can you trust that memory: what is memory: what is made up: when did you first make believe: imagine: when did you know: how did you trust yourself to tell your story: when did it happen: how long ago was it why does it feel fresh still: is this trauma: a close call: a retelling: a rumor: did you make it up along the way: exaggerate facts: did you call yourself out on it: did you remember: didn't you: how much did you remember: are we back at the beginning:

- *What sources can you trust?*

not that one:
that one there:
no one listens:
except the dead:
no one: listening:
the dead: the dead:
no one mourning:

- *What is your relationship to these sources?*

the simplest way of doing this: write what we miss:

- *What are your sources?*

I : imagine

- *How do you organize those sources?*

organize: loneliness :: sort: one absence: after another :: stack: one dearth: onto another dearth: dearth on death :: collate: the unmarked graves: arrange: my hands: around your heart: pumping :: compile: her father: there at her grave: crying out for her: lips wet with regret :: organize: a father: organize: another father: organize: them all: and tell them: what they matter:

- *What other sources might you use?*

candlelight: in abundance: the flickers: the dead: murmuring: we sing:

- *What other sources might you use?*

a chorus

- *What sources still need translating:*

: a step through your doorway

: a home

: jacaranda blossoms

: purpling your front yard

: the red and pink rose bushes

: bright

: the night blooming jasmine

: each flower: a star

: falling backward

SIX

the ground where our language suggests a body there is none

—Sara Lupita Olivares

The Road from My Mother's Womb

Loneliness is a wound I've inherited. I wail. She weeps. *You were*
    so alone in there, she cries, *you clawed yourself out.*

She traces my fingers along the ridges of her postpartum belly
    to remind me where I come from. Sometimes,

though, it feels like she wishes she could claw herself back in. More
    than the dead, we mourn the living but lost.

Abandoned, indefinitely. In an empty house, from flaccid breasts
    she nurses the ghosts of my brothers, only there's

nothing left. No one. Along the mud-strewn road on which I'll
    never return, I hear her cradle song. Off-key, she

sings the names of those forgotten. A dirge both past and prediction:
    the last name that trills from her mouth is my own.

Bautizo

On the film-thin skin of stagnant rainwater, beside the eggs of zancudos, I'm christened charco: he who searches in shallow pools for reflections of his father. Only, there are no fathers, just as there are no rivers, simply their beds cracked open with thirst. Still, my insatiable longing to know who or where I come from reverberates. I am an echo with no map. Because I prefer the dead—the named and unnamed—over the living, where I must go no directions exist. One trait I share with my ancestry is not ultimately whether we stay behind or leave forever: it is our restlessness. Alive or buried, it buzzes.

The River Coursing Through Us Is Dirty and Deep

And afterward, my mother pours stove-warmed water over
my back to console me for what I can't understand.

        I practice in a mirror what little Spanish I know.
        Slowly, my breath blurs my reflection into a fog.

                Every year I blew out the reused birthday candles as a child,
                I had hoped to become someone else, someone unrecognizable.

Our hands clasped together before bed, I become
more suspicious: I squint up and see strangers in prayer.

        I don't belong to my family, I convince myself. I take a vow
        of silence. I won't speak until I'm returned to my rightful family.

                I write my parents to explain to them how I know. They tell
                      me they understand. There is precedence for how I feel.

Both my grandfathers, I learn years later, convince
my parents as children that they were not theirs.

        From one day to the next they were fatherless,
        like so many other children in our family.

                Your father is gone. Gone away. Gone for good.
                Crossed over. Coming back. Nearby, but never close.

Before mine leaves, I barricade myself in my room to sniff
his fat wallet, wondering why he could never afford to love me.

        When he leaves and closes the door behind him, that sound
        echoes in the chambers of our hearts for generations.

            I hold my breath knowing how easily
            we can drown in what we don't know.

That birthday wish was the only
wish that's ever come true.

       Barely, I swim. Like an animal. My grandmother—were
       she alive—would scold me for floating in such filth.

Before

from Coxcatlán, San Luis Potosí to Matamoros, Tamaulipas

                                                      as in *before* el rio

                    as in *before* crossing

                          or before he fell asleep in his mother's arms
                          inside a toolshed overrun with field mice
                          their first night inside the United States

              I am wrong

what he means by before is a   *before*   barely imaginable

                        *

        with both hands   index to thumb

                     thumb to index
                             I frame a front door
                             through which he sees   *before*

       there   his mother builds a fire to cook their meals

               there   at her table they sit to eat warm bowls of beans

    but this   his voice trembles   *was before we had to leave*

                        *

  here   I stumble through the overgrowth
     now   of what was once his home

              coiled roots
                 endless brambles
            decades of tear-shaped
leaves fallen
       from the canopy

   she tried her best to protect me   *before*   *but she couldn't*

   they shielded me from my father's rage
            he murmurs
          almost to the trees

           *

     he tells me he had to   run
                 from this house

    he was convinced he says of his father *I was not his*

    first it was his words
   then   the belt
then his fists

              before

    he began with stones

          *

alone   at this house   his voice sounds dull

    distant

                a cassette that fits inside my palm

                         listening
                      I wonder
how many   befores
we've abandoned beginning here   in a jungle

                    where every utterance
every *before*   becomes   an echo

    leave   *he warns*   *before it gets too late*

           you'll be eaten alive

Detained

Before I am born my father is arrested. He knew
only one way to get into this country and when asked,
tried to bring his cousin in the same way too. I visit
him in jail. I reach out for his hand when the guard's
distracted, but he jerks away. Other times, when he calls,
I don't pick up. Though we only ever speak for a minute,
or two, it's too expensive—the hurt, the disappointment.
He sends pictures of himself from wherever he ends up
so I know where to find him. I find him, cradling his own
body when questioned by police. When given the chance
to make a call, he refused. Pride let him forget my mother
was home alone with three boys. I call my mother to ask
what year he was arrested. She tells me, *I was afraid he'd
never come back*. Days later, when he came back, he came
back with no answers. I ask how many days he spent in jail
and he says, *I don't remember*. I hang up. There is no one else,
no one who can remember. Sometimes it's me stuck in a cell.

Time Echoes Like Church Bells

I watch cowered in the back pews you being baptized in 1855 just after you lose both your parents to yellow fever my tongue fades from my mouth just before you are given your new name Juan de la Cruz Palma my mouth melts away I want to say I want to say you were being saved I try to convince myself I want to know who I am eleven years from now you'll be dead and with you your memory of who we were I can't keep up these mythologies I can't save you just as I can't save you from myself and somehow I've suckered you here to this very page only to admit the many lies I've told myself about who you were never the future because you died in the past where I will have forgotten who I am when I can't even save myself how many times now and in the future will I have forgotten who I am I apologize if I have let you down sorry is my favorite word sorry for not intervening sorry for my intrusion like the letter *r* I am bent over repentant one *r* for my past and one *r* for my future in those pews I tell you I have nothing to be sorry for soon I'll disappear back to the present I am guilty of being drawn to you I'm sorry and guilty of saying I'm sorry too many times the both of us side by side in prayer I am sorry I have disappeared you

Dear Fake Father and Fake Mother,

[it began, the language slanting toward the bottom corner of the page.] Let me go. I'm not yours.

You are not mine. I'm sorry for what I write, as hard to read as your illiterate mothers'

signatures wherever they scribbled their names. *[Every word trembled with fear.]* We have never

belonged to each other, and still the love I have for you both makes me foam at the mouth.

Chain me to the tree trunk for biting the breasts that feed me, I'm starving for two people I will

never know. You've given me only your names. So many nights in the a's and o's of your names

I tried to decipher who you were, only to hear those empty vowels say *somos tu familia*. So many

nights I stood over your bed as you slept, hoping you'd say during your night terrors who you both

are. Your bodies sweat drenched beneath the bed sheets, whitened by moonlight, you looked like wet

tissues. I won't cry for what I've never been given. *[a lie even then]* I'll leave the first chance I get.

[only I don't leave. I never leave. I stay for far too long.] Don't bother looking. Even if I was standing

right in front of you you wouldn't know who I was. I've learned from the best how to hide in plain sight.

NENE

But I am the kind of man who's abandoned his father.
How easy, my tongue. Not me. Never. No. I tell myself
I am not the kind of man who'd abandon his child. I can't
decide, should I love him or dump him—he won't miss
what's never loved him. What I know about fatherhood
is tidal, it comes and goes. What I know about fatherhood
does not yet ache. While we play peek-a-boo he gaggles.
I feed him milk from an unwashed bottle. Hmm. Because
he looks like me, I must look after him. *So helpless, so young*,
I convince myself; every baby needs a father. I swaddle
my father like a baby. No. I cuddle a baby who is my father.

Pesadilla

I dig up their graves and pin their corpses to a map, wings spread. I make them bearers of my many sins. My faults, I've concluded, are hereditary: diseased, dejected. Each of my flaws, their making. With idle hands I play with their lives as it pleases me. I rummage through their belongings: correspondence, journal entries, photos, birth and death certificates but the documents I uncover are as cheap as the paper this poem is printed on. I curate. Anthropologically, I designate their lives primitive, pathetic. The artifacts I appropriate I resurrect in my image: I'm certain I'm the most beautiful legacy they could have imagined. If they were more than peons, I would have been their muse. The mythologies I create are these poems I write. Full of holes. Unable to hold water. Not worth their weight. Blood is not thicker than water. The bodies of water my ancestors crossed diluted me. I will never know who I come from. I'm alone.

Partial Interview

Brownsville, Texas

We walk alongside the river,   and I, several feet from what we've last said to one another. I ask, softer than a desert breeze, did your   ever love you? When   stops and crosses   arms, I'm reminded why I've stopped asking questions.   don't remember where   crossed. Here. No, maybe there. If there is no beginning, here is no end. There, across the edge of the border, we watch a boy stare into another country. I stare at the boy, here. You'll never know what he sees,   says to me.   left   country like   father left me. What   carry in   blood, I made sure to never pass down. If you're wondering now, what   meant. Me too. When we continued to walk along the river, you could have confused its current for someone crying. It wasn't my   . It wasn't me. It was only

IN A DREAM MY FATHER HAS A STROKE

In the car, we argue over the last wrong turn he's made. My father refuses to admit he is lost. He tries to reassure me. *I know   where I'm   going*, he says, his words   slowly

                                                                                                                   wander

off   outside

                    the car window

                                                                  into an abandoned

                                                                                                lot

                                      overrun

              with dandelion

                                            the blossoms

                                                                         floating

back

                            in front

                                          of the windshield

                    on a spring

                                                  breeze

At the intersection   we slow   to a stop. I circle the car to open the driver door. I pull him from the car to lay him on the floor   his

body as light as a birthday wish   his eyes
shut tight   lips pursed   a still lit
candle   quivering   before its blown out.

Visiting my grandmother's grave, I visit her house in a dream

I kneel at her gravestone to cut back the grass that's crept over her name.
                                                                 At her doorstep, I knock.

It's been too many years since I've last come to visit her.
                                        She welcomes me. Tells me to sit by her bay window.

I pour water on the stone to remove dirt from her face. Slowly, she reappears.
                                      The sunlight beams through her house. She is just as I remember.

I sit down beside her grave and speak to her.
                                                  I thought you were dead abuelita, I say.

In the language she understands, I tell her who I have become.
                                        I carried you to your grave, abuelita, I tell her.

Soy poeta. Soy un professor. Soy padre.
                                                        Estas equivocado, she responds.

A flurry of leaves seems delighted. Then settles.
                                                      I want to touch her but hesitate.

As quiet as a goodbye. Reluctant.
                                                        The sunlight begins its slip into shadows.

I don't want to leave her, again.
                                      The skyline trembles violet. I know we are losing time

I don't know when I will be back.
                                                       ¿Puedo quedar contigo? I ask.

I place my palm against her cheek, the heat dissipates.
                                      No, she says. Esta casa solo es un recuerdo.

Cuéntame un cuento

In one version, my father swims across. In another,
he cannot. In one version, he drowns. In another,

                        he crosses on the shoulders of a cousin whose name
                        he can't remember. Between this version and another,

he has begun to lose his mind. Which is another way
of saying that when we look into one another's eyes,

                        I am rarely his son, and he was never my father. In one
                        version, I can't remember him, which is another way

of saying, sometimes, I forget. Forgive me for saying so
but memory is a bastard; it has no father or no mother.

                        Sometimes, the constant telling hurts in ways that have
                        little to do with pain. What's empty, grows emptier. No

more can come from another version when he is gone.
I can't keep track, the different and indifferent versions.

Layover / Overlay

from LAX to MEX to CUN

My mother wants to show me where she comes from. Only,
she isn't from here. Not *here*, here. The miles spent in flight,

the hours-long layover, she overlays everything we will see
with what she once saw. She translates from entonces to ahora:

the lighthouse of her parents' youth—decommissioned. The once
-humble pier, reaching through blue-watered memories—now

sargassum seaweed. On this flight, I am forty-six years behind
her. I've only visited Baja, the edges. But never the center, its

truth. I try to reconcile her memory the finger-smudged windows
in the taxi, in the port window's pinhole, in the residue of others

who've left one place for another.

~

                          My mother ~~wants to~~ shows me
where she comes from. Only, she isn't ~~from~~ here. She's not from

there, either. Nor then. In 1968, she boards a bus back to Mexico.
She is only twenty years old. With everything I've packed this

trip, I've forgotten where to begin. Not, *where were you born?*
Not, *where are you from?* I ask, *why did you travel back?* In time,

she remembers more than she will ever tell me. I would not want
to make you cry, she says. Not now. So, I overlay the dates of her

return with the Tlatelolco massacre. I imagine her curled up, dead, on the ground. I imagine her curled in a bus seat, near the driver,

reading and rereading instructions her mother has written. *Sit close to the driver. Talk to no one, especially men. Hug my mother for me*

as tightly as you can; I probably won't see her again.

~

My mother ~~wants to~~ shows me ~~where she comes from. Only~~, she isn't ~~from~~ here.

Not here, but there. In the country we've both longed for, and my mother has made into memory, she tells me this is where you belong.

It wasn't my country I missed, it was my people, she says. I take notes in my journal, careful not to say what I am not allowed to say.

Inside the 200-passenger flight of her memory where I am only a guest, I think *Then why did it take you so long to bring me here?*

Secuestro

It was a butcher knife   no   a small pistol   I don't know   she kept beneath her pillow   debajo de su almohada   cargada   descargada   beneath her bed inside   a nightstand drawer   sin filo   debajo de su almohada   afilado cargada   debajo de su almohada   unloaded   beneath the bed   sin filo dentro de un cajón   descargada   sobre la mesita de noche   beneath her pillow dormida   asustada en la noche   cargada   debajo de su almohada mis hermanos en la cama   con filo   sin filo   debajo de la cama dormidos asustados   al lado de una pistola   en la cama   cargada con miedo

[Memory] is a   space

on a birth certificate where a father's name should
                      go   goes,

      going   til gone.   more damming than   omission,
the admission: *un hijo espocito, un hijo natural, un hijo de la chingada,* etc.

etc. If [   ]   left, he took
         generations of fathers with him.   this

country is the failure to remember
       yourself   . My mother,   my brother's

names   dead, not dead dead, but dead
          dead   because we refuse to remember where

she comes from,   Guadalajara, or Mexicali,
      the dilapidated shack of [   ]   in. The home

     I grew my [   ], a telephone dangled from the wall,
disconnected.   I barely remember   the furniture

rearranged   .   this home   that home,   walls
   painted   blinding white,   the   blank space I

remember   where I come from
     moved.

                if [   ] could
     be   nowhere   no one.

               ? No.
                  [   ] is harder

than I imagine.

                        a   blank space   an ocean of white

I float in
        for lifetimes   to remember.

On a Good Day

she makes a list
of where she's
        lived:

address
    street name
every city & state:

the present
the past
    and where we've
        never lived.

*

where we've lived
    I plant memories:

honeysuckle
    jacaranda
        night-
blooming jasmine
        bougainvillea

where the hours
pass through the
sieve

of what she can no
longer remember.

*

she etches each
    house

over the parcel
    of her palm:

    a door with
no knob

a broken window
    without a wall

        a garden
with no soil

*

in a parking lot
    inside a
laundromat

    I smell the meal
    she's prepared
innumerable times

clavo sal comino
oja de laurel
        pimienta

    the spices she
tastes but cannot
        name

*

Exhalar

exhale: ya lo pasado, pasado no me interesa

exhale: progreso, palenque, guadalajara, mexicali, coxcatlán, matamoros

exhale: jacaranda blossoms and rose petals intermingling in the breeze

exhale: the smell of mezquinos being singed from your whole body

exhale: the living that nightly linger in every one of your dreams

exhale: the mystery of your father's father he took to his grave

exhale: ya olvide, ya olvide

exhale: your corrugated tongue that speaks past and present

exhale: brownsville, los ángeles, chicago, plano, torrance, long beach

exhale: the body of your brother floating face-up in a swimming pool

exhale: the grave you sold beside your mother when you needed money

exhale: the loved ones, the living and dead, who refuse to visit

exhale: the bones you've undug to suck their marrow

exhale: inhale

Through the Snow

I stare through a photo until it blurs. My mother, a child
in a parade of parishioners, afraid, has just begun to cry.
Bewildered, she stretches out her arm for her mother or
father who stand, I assume, out of frame. Lost, the both
of us, through time, I wonder if we'll find who we look for,
who we've been separated from. Winter in New Hampshire,
so far from family, no one here seems to notice the trees
have no branches, and the deer that graze beneath the snow
are indifferent. Deep in the meadow before it becomes
a forest, I lose my way. A panic breaks into my body that
belongs to us both. She's lost her parents just as one day,
miles from these pines, I'll lose mine. I look for home not
certain of a direction. Lost and scared, time is a snowfall
I can barely see through. In the mass of strangers, I kneel
in front of her. I remind her, us both, we are never alone.

DISCULPA

~~I've tended to all~~ the wronged graves, ~~stepped through the wronged cemeteries~~ centuries.

~~I was only nineteen~~ when you died.

I am sorry. ~~Was sorry.~~ Sorry, still.

~~I've turned to strangers, strange places, instead of you. A betrayal.~~

~~I felt you died young, just seventy-nine years old.~~

~~Twenty-two years, ten months, and six days later,~~ I bring my son to meet you.

~~With so few memories,~~ I pursue you in photos, through papers, in artifacts.

~~The last time we touched,~~ my lips to your forehead, your body was ocean cold.

July, 22, 2023

My memories of you, younger still, are slowly dying.

~~You were only one bridge, one half hour away.~~

Strange, I know more about you now, after your death.

~~I've mourned both you and my memories.~~

~~Then, I moved. Then I moved even further away.~~

~~Seven months and ten days old,~~ I make him a promise.

~~The only difference~~ between an apology and a promise is the degree of hope.

September 16, 2000

He will know you more than I ever did.

Guadalajara

My grandmother came to this city in 1941 to marry.
My mother was born here in 1948. Between choice
(or lack of choice) and circumstance, inside the half-
way point, I'm only here by chance: to walk my son
through the plaza at dawn because he cannot sleep.
At this hour, through the conferences of men laying
on sidewalks, I text my mother, where *exactly* were
 you born? *Here. Maybe there*, she replies. I pull up
a map to look for any cross streets, the intersections
of time we might pass through. *I don't know exactly*,
she clarifies days later. Seventy-one years behind, I
point out to my son anything I can make landmark:
the pigeons' incessant circles, last night's trash bags
left piled on street corners, rows of shoeshine stands
chained and locked up, the once-busy chairs that seem
at this hour, forever empty. Soon, we will depart this
this place and never return: the first of many cities he

will leave, just as the past has left us with the litanies

of indifferent cities we will faintly remember as ours.

Hogar

es el desamor del que nos protegemos

distancia suficiente para alejarnos—

la consecuencia, de la cual, que terminamos

solos. Solitarios. Soledad lo suficientemente

profunda para ahogarnos en ella. Hasta los tobillos:

hasta las rodillas: hasta la cintura: hasta el cuello—

sumergido, incapaz de nadar, pretendo no tener miedo.

Trago agua contra mi voluntad porque el duelo es una marea.

La llamo Proserpina. La llamo Victoria.

La llamo por los vivos que están en la orilla, incapaces de entrar,

que se niegan a salvarme, porque ya no o nunca me amaban.

Antes:

antes del río:

antes de que el río sangre:

antes de que el río se desangre:

antes de que el río se desangre en el mar—

intento amar lo suficientemente profundo,

a través de donde reside la oscuridad:

mi lenguaje: burbujas sobrellenadas de luz.

Notes

The opening quote is from Derek Walcott's poem, "To the Hotel Saint Antoine" from his collection *The Gulf and Other Poems*.

The epigraph for Section I is taken from Sara Uribe's book, *Antígona González*.

"Those Graves" is inspired by Larry Levis' poem "Those Graves in Rome" from his book *Winter Stars* and John Murillo's poem, "Flowers for Etheridge" from his book, *Up Jump the Boogie*.

The quatrain referenced in "Those Graves" and translated from the Spanish by the author was written by poet, Manuel José Quintana, from a much longer poem titled, "Despedida de la juventud."

The epigraph for Section III is taken from Valeria Luiselli's collection of essays, *Sidewalks*.

Canto for My Love Language is a cento that borrows lines from the following songs: *Amor eterno / Quererte a ti / Deja que salga la luna / El jinete / Cucurucucu paloma / Mi viejo / Besame mucho / Cielo rojo / Perdon / Se te olvida*

"Emancipación" is inspired by Natasha Trethewey's "The Southern Crescent," from her book *Native Guard* and Geoffrey Davis', "King County Metro" from his collection *Revising the Storm*.

The epigraph for Section VI is taken from Sara Lupita Olivares' poem "To Watch" from her collection *Migratory Sound*.

The title "The River Coursing Through Us is Dirty and Deep" is borrowed from CD Wright's poem "Everything good between men and women."

Acknowledgments

Thanks to the editors of the following publications in which these poems, some of them in earlier versions, have appeared:

"Leaving Home, 1986" and "Leaving Home in Reverse, 1986" *Copper Nickel*

"On Visiting Mexico City, 2014" *The Normal School*

"Topography," *Zócalo Public Square*

"Cancún, 1978," *Salt*

"Vestiges," *Academy of American Poets*, Poem-a-Day series

"A Child of Immigrants" and "Burials," *The Adroit Journal*

"Mourning," *Ninth Letter*

"Kindling" and "An Emptied House," *Prairie Schooner*

"Luto," *Puerto del Sol*

"Herencia" and "La Bestia (1945)," *Rejected Lit Magazine*

"Thirteen Years Old (1934)," "Piramide de Hombres (1943)," "Thirteen Years Old (1961)," and "Bautizo," *Waxwing Literary Journal*

"Emancipación (Nov 1941)" *Missouri Review*

"Las Lavanderas (c. 1945)" *Gulf Coast*

"Sin Zapatos (1948)" and "Those Flowers" *The Offing*

"Hotel Moreno (1959)," *Crab Orchard Review*

"Detained," "Cuentame un cuento," and "[Memory] is a space," *Michigan Quarterly Review*

"Nene," *Sonora Review*

"Partial Interview," *fugue journal*

Gratitude

To the poets and writers who have helped shape these poems and helped make this collection:

Jamaica Baldwin, Jordan Charlton, Claire Jimenez, Jess Poli, Katie Mayra, Ava Winter, Kwame Dawes, Grace Bauer, Tom Gannon, Amelia María de la Luz Montes, Luis Othoniel Rosa Rodriguez, Amy Hassinger, Janice Harrington, Irvin Hunt, Brett Kaplan, Corey Van Landingham, Michael Torres, Diana Marie Delgado, Julia Bouwsma, and Liz Harms.

To the following individuals, whose boundless generosity has nurtured my poetry and nourished my life, immeasurable respect and resounding love: Sara Borjas, Saddiq Dzukogi, and Ivan Young.

To my family—living and dead—who have put up with my questions, my curiosities, and who have willingly and unwillingly recalled memories to help me find my way back: les amo profundamente.

To Janett Barragán Miranda, once again and always, for your love and for making us a family.